THE
FORGOTTEN
SOCIETY

This is one of those drawings that come to life.
I love it as I love the old men in it. It is
here, it is when I draw that know one draws
better.

97 come here from Italy (Sicily) 1894 married in 1914
arrive duce' Roma. I can sing better than
Arthur Godfrey. I use to sing years ago
did you ever hear C So lo mi o. You never
hear this whole song.

8 Feb. 1973

THE FORGOTTEN SOCIETY

92 drawings by
ALAN E. COBER

Dover Publications, Inc., New York

Published in Canada by General Publishing Company, Ltd., 30 Lesmill Road, Don Mills, Toronto,
Ontario.
Published in the United Kingdom by Constable
and Company, Ltd., 10 Orange Street, London WC 2.

The Forgotten Society is a new work, first published by Dover Publications, Inc., in 1975.

International Standard Book Number: 0-486-21405-2
Library of Congress Catalog Card Number: 74-76981

Manufactured in the United States of America
Dover Publications, Inc.
180 Varick Street
New York, N.Y. 10014

To my father,
Sol Walter Cohen

Publisher's Note

Alan E. Cober is an artist who derives his inspiration from life, a classicist and realist in the graphic tradition that extends from Dürer to George Grosz. His work stems from the same feeling of commitment that informs Goya's *Disasters of War* and Ben Shahn's Sacco-Vanzetti reportage.

Mr. Cober's father was a criminal lawyer for 48 years until his death in the spring of 1974. The young artist closely observed his father's activities, gaining firsthand knowledge of courtrooms, police work and detention of criminals. This experience quickened his interest in social inequities and the dark side of life.

The drawings in the present collection concern not only these courtroom and prison situations, but also other facets of Cober's social involvement: studies of old age homes and of Willowbrook, an institution for the mentally retarded, children and adults. This is the "forgotten" society that the artist records with both objectivity and sympathy.

Cober was born in New York City in 1935. He grew up in the Bronx, and attended public schools in Manhattan and the Bronx. In 1952 he was at a prep school in Riverdale, the Barnard School for Boys. From 1952 to 1954 he studied at the University of Vermont. Art school followed—the School of Visual Arts—until late 1956. There he studied with Al Werner, who instilled in him the importance of drawing and seeing; Robert Frankenberg and Howard Simon also influenced him at that time.

Cober was drafted into the Army in April 1958. After basic training at Fort Dix, N. J., he spent the rest of his two years teaching officers and heading the graphics department at the Special Warfare School, Fort Bragg, N. C. The group of men at that school were all well educated; handpicked by the Department of the Army, they included teachers, lawyers, writers, artists, Fulbright scholars and State Department personnel. Cober spent those two years drawing and learning; that is where he feels he received his real education.

Leaving the service, Cober freelanced, building his reputation and his style. Among the magazines that have published his work are *Sports Illustrated*, *Life*, *Redbook*, *McCall's*, *Parents Magazine*, the *Saturday Review*, the *Saturday Even-*

ing Post and *Time*. His interest in reportage was renewed in 1971, when *Newsweek* commissioned a series of drawings on prison life. Then *Look* commissioned him to go to Cambridge, Mass., to draw Daniel Ellsberg for the article "Ellsberg Speaks" (October 1971). In February 1972 he convinced the *New York Times* Op-Ed page to send him to Willowbrook to do drawings. They needed two; he did fifty. Cober has investigated the plight of the aged on his own.

As an illustrator-artist Cober has received over 200 different awards, including:

> Artist of the Year, 1965—Artists Guild of N.Y.
> Gold medals, 1969, 1971, 1974—Society of Illustrators
> Gold medal, 1974—Art Directors Club, N.Y.
> Gold medal, 1971—Art Directors Club, Washington, D.C.
> Gold medal, 1971—Art Directors Club, Chicago
> Audubon Artists Medal for Creative Graphics, 1971
> John Taylor Arms Award for Creative Graphics, Audubon Artists, 1972

Cober has also been represented in many national drawings shows, such as "A Century of American Illustration" at the Brooklyn Museum, 1972. Two of the children's books for which he has done pictures have been among the *New York Times* ten best illustrated books, in 1968 and 1969.

Mr. Cober, his wife Ellen and their children Leslie and Peter live in a 170-year-old house filled with American folk art.

THE
FORGOTTEN
SOCIETY

6 May 1973

1

Mrs Erhard visits Miss McGinnis and tells her she's not going anywhere - they've been friends for years and years. She nods to me as to say don't listen to her because she doesn't know what she's talking about.

She's waiting for a cab to take her home. She's been there 2 years. "You take two flower pots I'll take the others. I'll have to borrow some money from Miss Kelly because I forgot my pocket book." You check my credit. You'll see that its good. Aren't you one of the Callahan boys? I don't like your beard." If you were better looking without it." (She has never seen me before.)

Alan E. Cober
9 June 1972.
Miss McGinnis

Alan E. Cober
Camp Salomon
14 Sept. 1972

3

4

5

16 Feb 1973

8

FIFTY
years from
Mailer SAFCO
+ started as office boy

GREAT DAY
VALDERI
HEVNU SHACH
HARTZA ALMU
ACHLONALE

Alan E. Gales
Singing m playing
OIFN DRIPETCHUK
Camp Salomon
14 Sept 1972

9

"Do you have any candy" No. I have no candy! Do you have some candy for the kids. I already gave them some. You're the fellow with the high tenor voice. Me? I can tell by your voice you're the one. I know! You got any candy in the box. I can't find the box. We'll look for it later. I'd like some butter scotch candy. You like butter scotch always liked it. What a memory you have to remember all this time. You mean 85 years? No, silly 20 years or so. How old are you now? I just had my 28th birthday. Daddy are you down stairs? Your daddy just left for work on the trolley. Oh!

9 June 1972
Loretta 93 years old

10

11

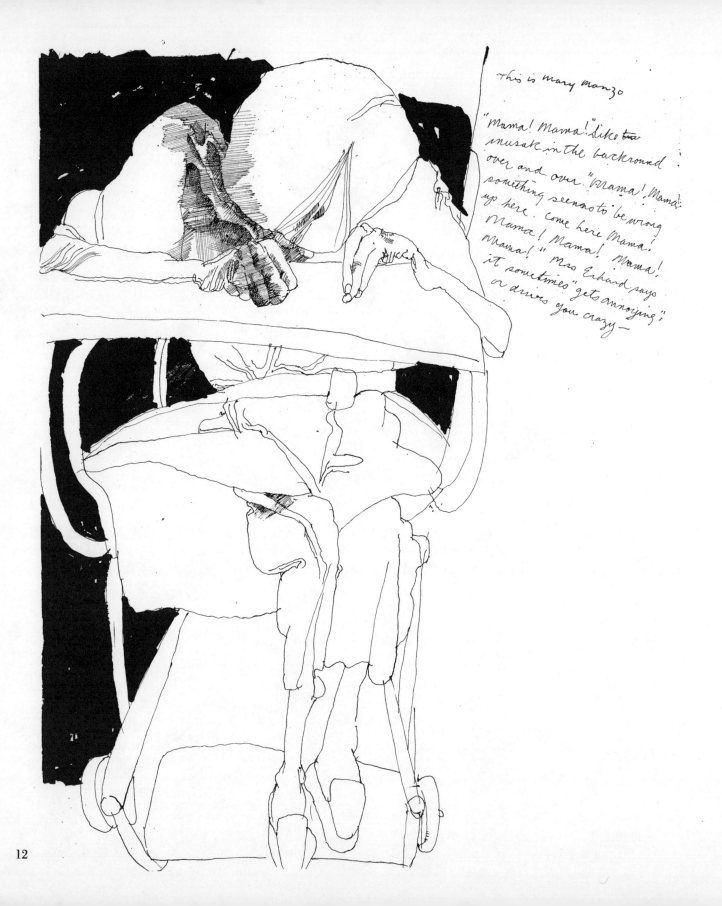

This is mary manzo

"Mama! Mama! Like the
musak in the backround
over and over "mama! mama!
something seems to be wrong
up here. come here Mama!
Mama! Mama! Mama!
Mama!" Mrs Eckard says
"it sometimes "gets annoying"
or drives you crazy—

12

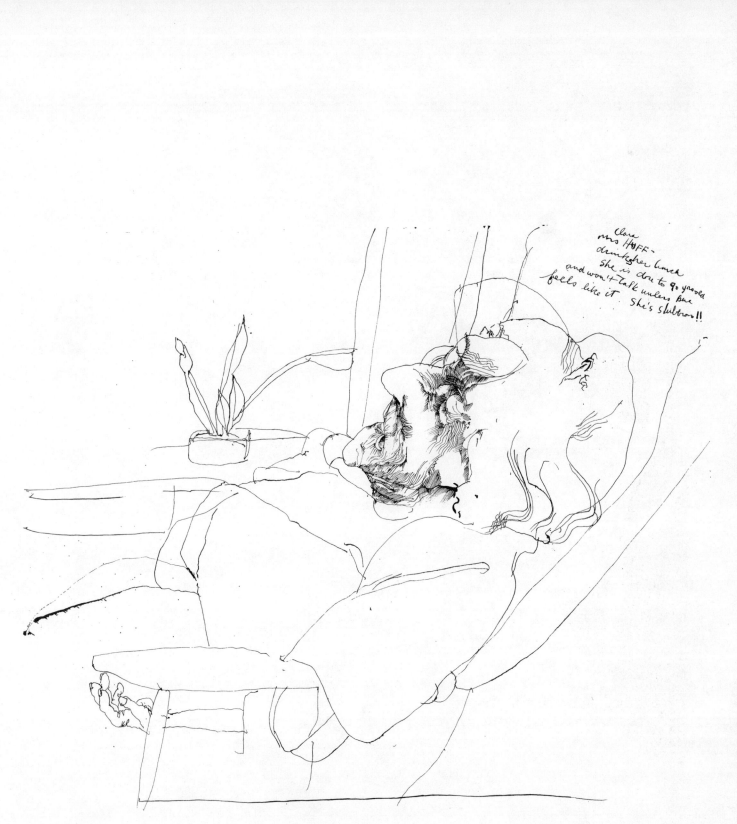

Clara
Mrs HUFF -
drinks her lunch
She is due to go gravel
and won't talk unless she
feels like it. She's stubborn!!

13

Mr Lyman Pollock
age 69.
Retired plumber from Danvers
Cape Cod, Mass, 3 July 1972

14

99 years old.
born Apr 4 1874
County Home
10 Aug 1972

old time fisherman
Richard Johnson
age 64.

16

"Those damnable young
men and their
balconies"

Alan E. Cohen
24 Dec. 1972
My Father has a bad
back

4.9 Majorchad 1972
210 E. 15th St.
My Father
Sol Walter Cohen

18

19

29 July 1972

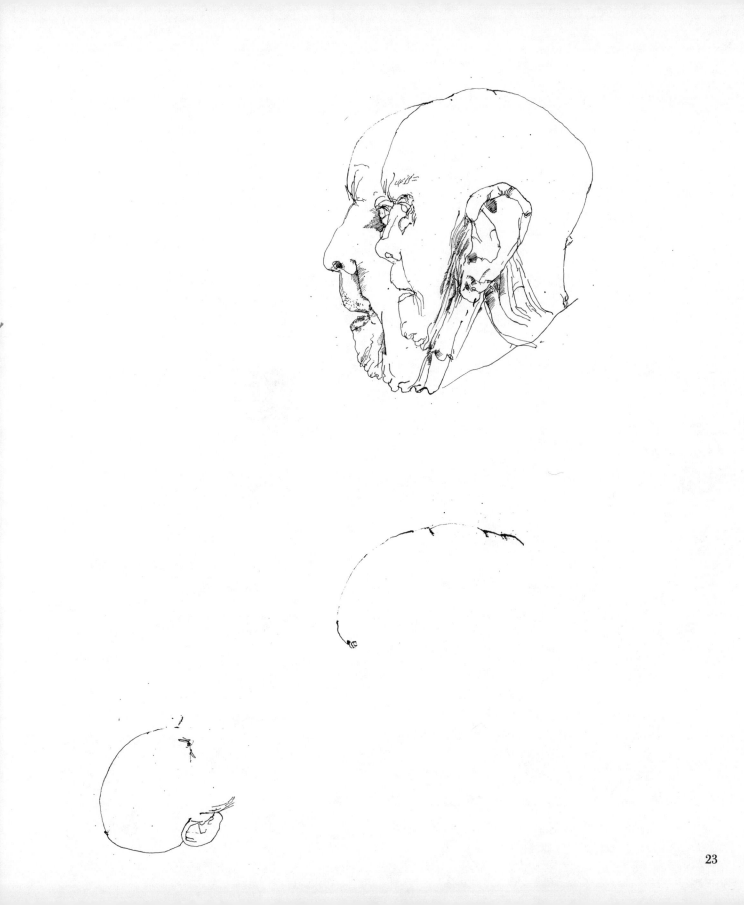

Wattledge Nursing home
30 May 1972
MRs Fay who she says she is
20 years old.

25

Her Husband was 32nd degree
mason

12 Jan 1973

married age 16 in Kentucky
Sadie Hamilton Bady aged 86
a good strong woman

27

Ralph McConkey 87
Born on Dale near
Ossining

29

Miss Fowler spouts poetry all day.
My luck she is not talking today
and I have a
tape recorder.
87 years old
she teaches school
sometimes each day.

31

NO EATING IN CLINIC AREA
NO SMOKING
HOSPITAL QUIET

33

a married couple
at Daughters of Jacob
Geriatric Center
11 Sept 1972

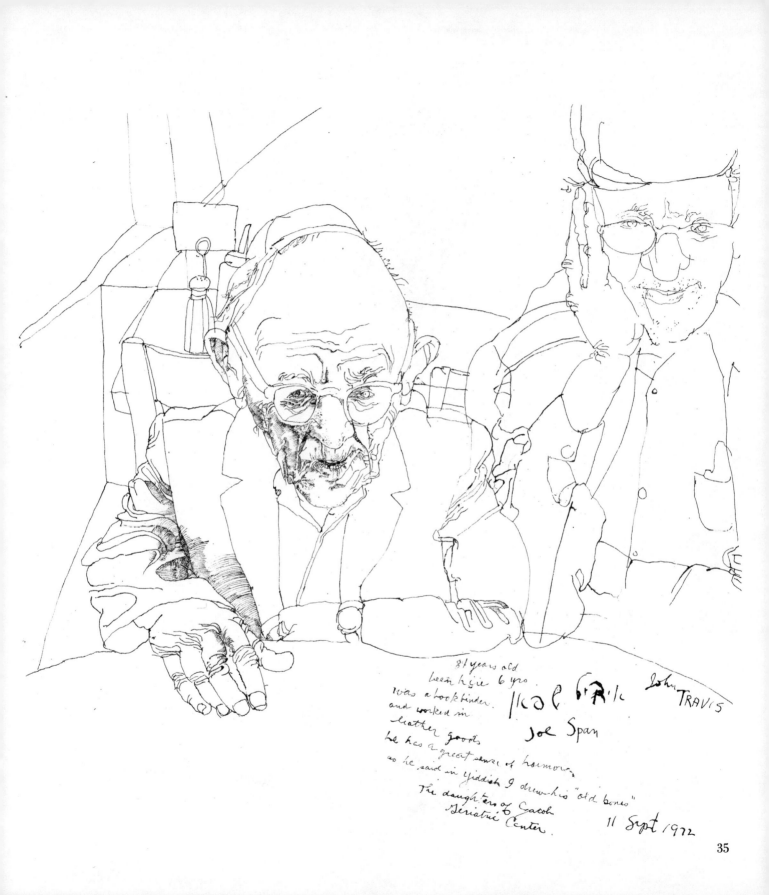

81 years old
been here 6 yrs.
was a bookbinder.
and worked in
leather goods
he has a great sense of humour
as he said in Yiddish I drew his "old bones"
The daughters of Jacob
Geriatric Center.

Joe Span

John TRAVIS

11 Sept 1972

35

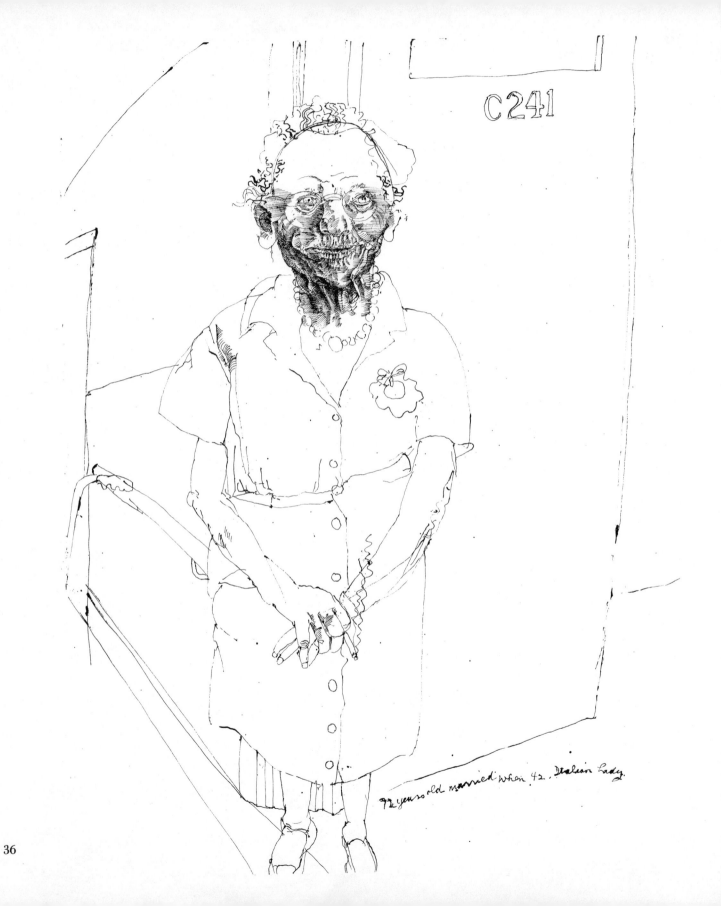

C241

92 years old married when 42. Italian Lady.

22 Dec 1972
Alan E. Cober

mrs Ray say she is 20 year old
and if this is a drawing of her
husband. this was my orientation
to the aged. I met a 97 year
old woman (blind) from Flatbush
Brooklyn she sayoohe is now
on display like a
monkey

Yes No Yes No Yes No
Yes No Yes No
Yes No Yes No
Yes No
Yes No

40

I'm 85 years old
and I'm waiting to die!
My birthday is in
two weeks. I came from
Germany in 1911. Munich.
I traveled to many places
but when my wife caught me
I was trapped. I never traveled
again. I never will. I'm waiting
to die.

22 Dec 1872

41

16 Febr 1973

The Daughter of Jacob
Geriatric Center
11 Sept 1972

43

44

Miss Getz

Mrs Scheming

For a half an hour I drew mrs Scheming getting the impression she didn't know I was there
drawing. Someone walked by and asked her "why she didn't smile for the man" let alone
that "If he told me who he was and that he wanted me to smile I would have smiled" she said
"I fainted".

Alan E. Cober
2 June 1972
Westedge Nursing.

48

Arthur E. Colin
16 Feb 1973

Alan E. Cober
15 Feb 1973

To Say the very very least the Stench is nauseating (there is a smell killer but the institution has run out of funds to buy it!) the sight is shocking, to see the emaciated bodies lying like infants on wheeled cots is not believable if you've never experienced it. the man on the right is 42 years old and is shaved once a week. He has be here less than a year. coming from home where his mother cared for him until she died. the boy on the left is 19 years can walk. talk. feed themselves are toilet trained. They all react in some way to affection. Many of these boys? could have been trained if they had been institutionalized at infancy. the institution is doing this now in the infant center through therapy. education and love.

People keep asking me if I was depressed by seeing all this. No, the thing is positive. This ward isn't positive but who's fault is it? certainly not this institution's!

52

Female
between Adult ward
Mongolian, Micro, and under developed inmate (I.Q. 3)
Willowbrook State School
March, 1972   Alan E. Cober

57

58

these boys. are 3 of maybe 40 there are able to sit in wheel chairs on the severely spastic ward. They make a variety of sounds and have a variety of habits such as chewing on a rag, or swallowing and regurgitating their food and reswallowing it etc. They bob their heads and scream and cry. They basically sit all day in line of 20 facing the other 20.

occupational therapy at Willowbrook State School, Staten Island, N.Y. There are 3 mongoloids ages 23, 11, 9 . . . . The next step would be to the wood working shop. 9 March 1972 drawn E. Coker

Mt Sinai Hospital
Intensive Care Unit
13 Sept 1972

63

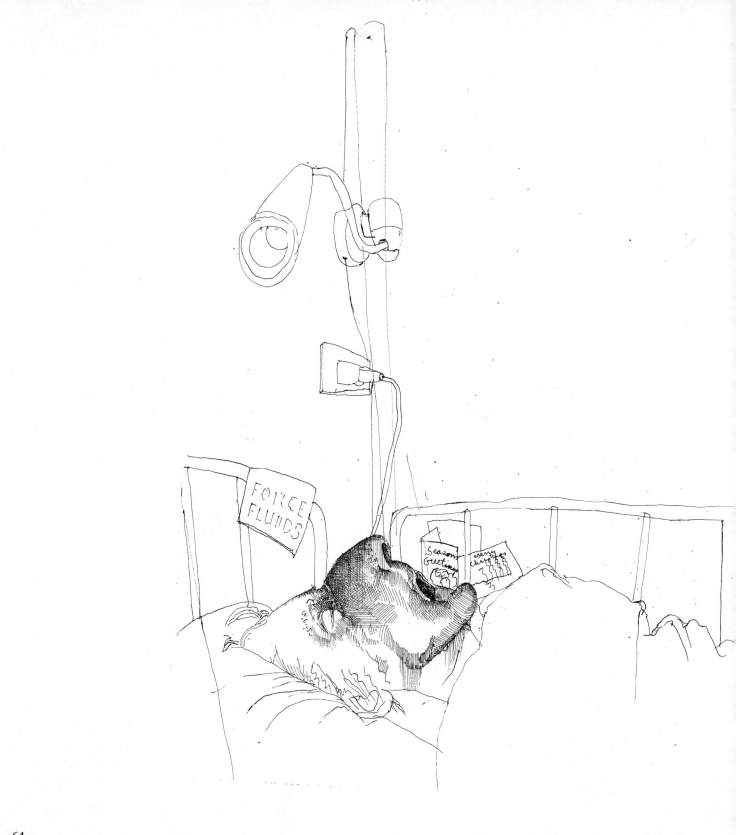

The average IQ is 20. the biggest is about 40. the old is age is 77. the man on the right is 66. the man on the left is about 35 His IQ is 34

68

cooking Ray.
Patterson

73

Alan E Cohen
4 Feb 1971
17th Precinct
Detention Cells.

74

Alan E. Cohen
Judge Edwards
1A1
Arraignment Court
9 Feb 1971

Criminal Courts Building
Arraignment—Alan T. Color
1 Feb 1971

79

Waverly Center for Soc
Services
Alan E. Cohen
29 Sept 1972

The Barrier
keeps the clients and workers apart

81

alan E. Coes
Legal Aid Society
during Arraignments
2 Feb 1971

Alan E. Cober
Reception at Tombs
Prison N.Y.C.
3 Feb 1971

Alan E. Cohen
Panther Trial
officer white on stand
4 Feb 1971

85

Conference During the
Panther trial 4 Feb 19.71
Criminal Courts Building
Alan E. Cober

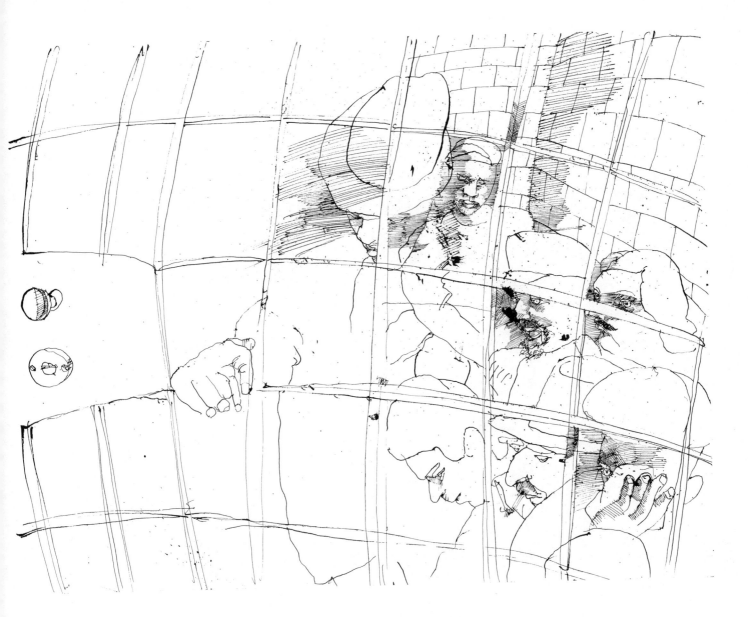

91

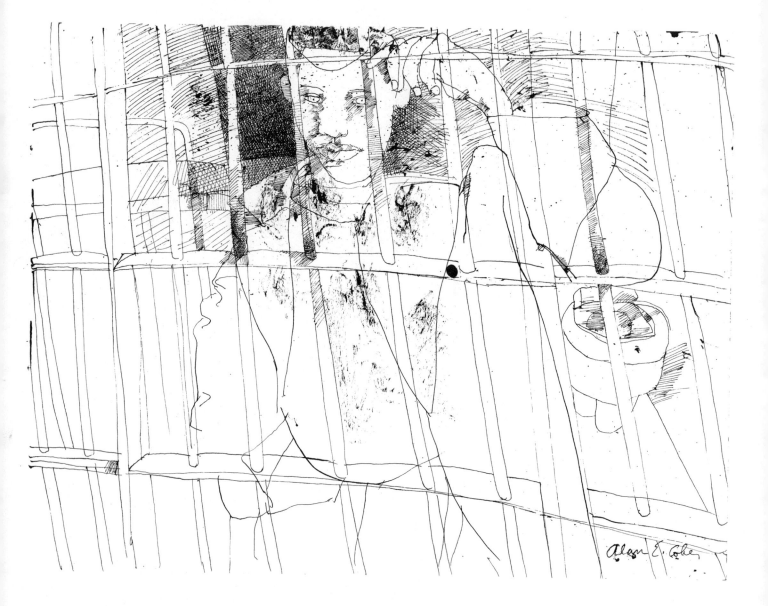

94

At the time of this drawing there are three men on death row Cell Block "K" at Greenhaven. Execution is limited to crimes committed involving the killing of a police officer or inmate while under life sentence. The inmates are incarcerated in seperate condemned cells.

The first execution in this chair was at Auburn July 7, 1891. This chair was moved last month from Sing Sing in Ossining N.Y. where 9 ewe.

Alan E. Cober

Electric chair
Greenhaven Prison
Stormville N.Y.
26 Feb 1971

95